11/14

NFL TODAY

THE STORY OF THE

NEW YORK JETS

NFL TODAY

THE STORY OF THE NEW YORK JETS

JIM WHITING

CREATIVE EDUCATION

PUBLISHED BY CREATIVE EDUCATION
P.O. BOX 227, MANKATO, MINNESOTA 56002
CREATIVE EDUCATION IS AN IMPRINT OF THE CREATIVE COMPANY
WWW.THECREATIVECOMPANY.US

DESIGN AND PRODUCTION BY BLUE DESIGN
ART DIRECTION BY RITA MARSHALL
PRINTED IN THE UNITED STATES OF AMERICA

PHOTOGRAPHS BY CORBIS (DAVID BERGMAN, LOUIE
PSIHOYOS/SCIENCE FACTION) GETTY IMAGES
(BRIAN BAHR, AL BELLO, DAVID BERGMAN/SPORTS
ILLUSTRATED, TIM CLARY/AFP, JAMES DRAKE/
SPORTS ILLUSTRATED, DAVID DRAPKIN, FOCUS ON
SPORT, HARRY HOW, MARK KAUFFMAN/TIME & LIFE
PICTURES, NICK LAHAM, LONNIE MAJOR/ALLSPORT,
JIM MCISAAC, VIC MILTON/NFL, RONALD C. MODRA/
SPORTS IMAGERY, NFL, DARRYL NORENBERG/NFL,
BERNIE NUNEZ, AL PEREIRA, AL PEREIRA/NEW YORK
JETS, RICH SCHULTZ, COREY SIPKIN/NY DAILY
NEWS ARCHIVE, RICK STEWART, KEVIN TERRELL,
ROB TRINGALI/SPORTSCHROME, JIM TURNER/NFL,
CHARLES AQUA VIVA, LOU WITT/NFL)

LIBRARY OF CONGRESS CATALOGING-IN-PUBLICATION DATA
WHITING, JIM.
THE STORY OF THE NEW YORK JETS / BY JIM WHITING.
P. CM. — (NFL TODAY)
INCLUDES INDEX.
SUMMARY: THE HISTORY OF THE NATIONAL FOOTBALL LEAGUE'S
NEW YORK JETS, SURVEYING THE FRANCHISE'S BIGGEST STARS
AND MOST MEMORABLE MOMENTS FROM ITS INAUGURAL SEASON
IN 1960 TO TODAY.
ISBN 978-1-60818-313-5
1. NEW YORK JETS (FOOTBALL TEAM)—HISTORY—JUVENILE
LITERATURE. I. TITLE.

GV956.N37W45 2013
796.332'64097471—DC23   2012033812

FIRST EDITION
9 8 7 6 5 4 3 2 1

COVER: TACKLE D'BRICKASHAW FERGUSON
PAGE 2: DEFENSIVE TACKLE SIONE POUHA
PAGES 4–5: QUARTERBACK JOE NAMATH
PAGE 6: WIDE RECEIVER JUSTIN MCCAREINS

TABLE OF CONTENTS

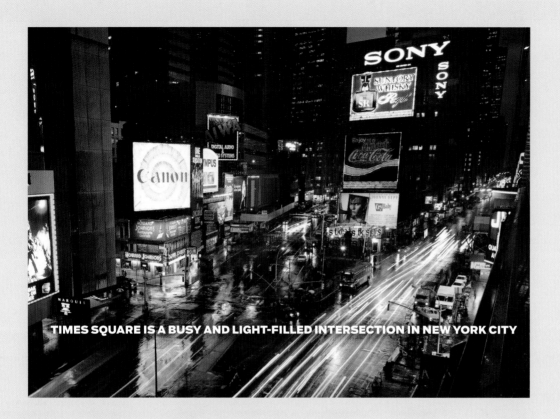

TIMES SQUARE IS A BUSY AND LIGHT-FILLED INTERSECTION IN NEW YORK CITY

Birth of the Titans

New York is famous for many things—perhaps most of all the towering skyscrapers that made it one of the world's first vertical cities. So it's ironic that its most famous nickname, "The Big Apple," originated in a humble horse stable hundreds of miles away. Sports reporter John Fitz Gerald is generally credited with coining the name in the early 1920s. Fitz Gerald especially liked horse racing, and he wrote, "The Big Apple. The dream of every lad that ever threw a leg over a thoroughbred and the goal of all horsemen. There's only one Big Apple. That's New York." The term came to him when he overheard two men walking their horses around a stable in New Orleans. One asked the other where he was heading next. "The Big Apple," was the proud reply.

A similar pride animated former broadcaster Harry Wismer in 1960 as he and the other founders of the fledgling American Football League (AFL) mounted a challenge to the older, well-established National Football League (NFL). The AFL put a team in New

FULLBACK BILL MATHIS WAS AN ALL-PRO FOR THE TITANS IN 1961

Don Maynard

WIDE RECEIVER / TITANS/JETS SEASONS: 1960–72 / HEIGHT: 6 FEET / WEIGHT: 180 POUNDS

When coach Sammy Baugh was putting together the first roster for the New York Titans in 1960, he remembered fellow Texan Don Maynard, a fleet-footed receiver then playing football in Canada. Baugh convinced team owner Harry Wismer to sign Maynard to the team's first contract. For the next 13 years, Maynard would play a vital role in the New York offense. During 5 of those seasons, he caught 50 or more passes for more than 1,000 yards each year. Maynard was renowned for his ability to improvise on the field. He would find a way to get open, even in the tightest coverage. Then he would use his outstanding speed to catch up with tosses from the team's quarterback. Once quarterback Joe Namath joined the Jets in 1965, the Namath-to-Maynard combination became one of the most lethal in the AFL. The pair clicked for two touchdowns in the AFL Championship Game in 1968, including the game winner. When Maynard retired in 1973, he held pro football records for career catches (633) and receiving yards (11,834).

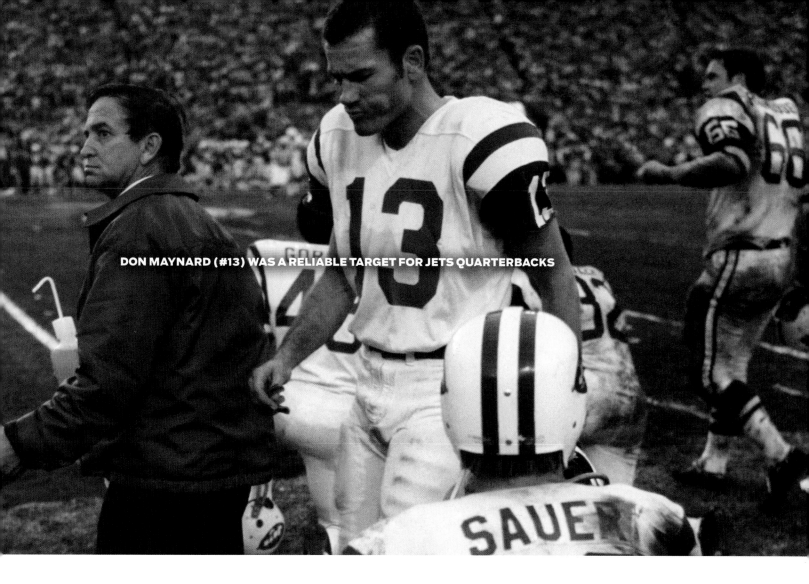

DON MAYNARD (#13) WAS A RELIABLE TARGET FOR JETS QUARTERBACKS

York, and Wismer became the owner of the New York Titans. Wismer immediately challenged the Giants, the city's NFL team, by proclaiming, "We're called Titans because titans are bigger than giants."

The Titans posted a respectable 7–7 record their first year, with a potent offense that revolved around quarterback Al Dorow and receivers Art Powell and Don Maynard. Maynard became the team's first star. With his outstanding speed and elusive moves, he scored 88 touchdowns during his career (still a club record) and eventually earned a place in the Pro Football Hall of Fame.

Unfortunately, the Titans struggled at the ticket office. Part of the problem was their home venue, the aging Polo Grounds (where baseball's New York Giants had played before moving to San Francisco in 1958). Average home attendance the first season was about 15,000, and 2 years later it dwindled to just over 5,000. Wismer couldn't pay players' salaries, and a group led by former television executive David "Sonny" Werblin purchased the franchise.

"He comes to play, and he comes to win."

DON MAYNARD ON JOE NAMATH

Werblin gave the club a complete makeover, changing its name to the peppier-sounding Jets and replacing the players' drab blue-and-gold uniforms with brighter kelly green and white. He also brought in veteran coach Weeb Ewbank. Ewbank, who had led the Baltimore Colts to two NFL championships, didn't try to fire up players by yelling at them. "Weeb Ewbank treated us like men, and I appreciated that," recalled center John Schmitt.

Despite their losing record (5–8–1) in 1963, Ewbank's Jets began building fan support. The fans had even more to cheer about the next season when the team moved to Shea Stadium in the New York City borough of Queens and featured a new star, 1964 AFL Rookie of the Year running back Matt Snell.

The excitement reached a fever pitch in 1965 when flashy quarterback Joe Namath arrived from the University of Alabama. Werblin convinced Namath to join the AFL instead of the NFL by offering him a 3-year contract for the then amazing sum of $427,000, making him the highest-paid American athlete in any sport. With his good looks and cocky attitude, "Broadway Joe" became a star both on the field and off.

Namath's teammates weren't jealous of the attention Broadway Joe commanded. Instead, they were impressed by the quarterback's work ethic. "He paid the price," said Maynard. "He worked just as hard and studied just as much film as anybody else. In that way, naturally, you accept the guy for what he does. He comes to play, and he comes to win."

Titan-ic Troubles

When the AFL was established in 1960, most of its franchises' owners were wealthy businessmen. That was not true of Titans owner Harry Wismer, a fast-talking sports broadcaster known for occasionally stretching the truth. During his three years as owner, the team was a financial bust. The club scrounged for practice fields and played home games before tiny crowds in the decaying Polo Grounds. To reduce expenses, Wismer stopped paying many bills, including hotel tabs and salary checks. Frustrated players finally took a stand in 1962, refusing to board the plane for an away game in Denver unless their salaries were guaranteed. That was one reason why offensive tackle Alex Kroll wrote, "The Titans of '62 stand unchallenged as the worst-managed, most-unprofessional professional team of the modern era." Eventually, the league took over the Titans to ensure that the AFL kept a team in New York. Despite his financial woes and questionable behavior, Wismer had several positive effects. He used his newspaper contacts to boost coverage for the league. Much more importantly, he originated the concept of revenue sharing, in which all eight teams received an equal amount of money from the league's television contract.

AL DOROW WAS THE FIRST QUARTERBACK FOR THE NEW YORK TITANS

Namath proved he was worth every penny. In 1966, he led the Jets to a 6–6–2 record by throwing long bombs to Maynard and second-year receiver George Sauer Jr. Everything was looking bright for the Jets until Namath began struggling with knee problems.

Namath played through the pain the next year, leading the Jets to their first winning record (8–5–1) and becoming the first quarterback in either the AFL or NFL to pass for more than 4,000 yards in a season. Rookie running back Emerson Boozer, meanwhile, paired with Snell to give New York perhaps the AFL's best rushing duo. The Jets were ready to soar.

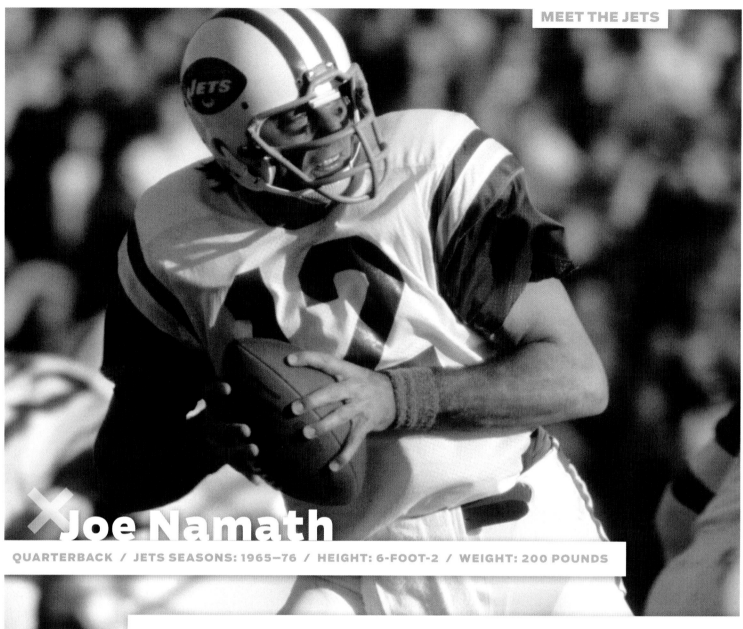

Joe Namath

QUARTERBACK / JETS SEASONS: 1965–76 / HEIGHT: 6-FOOT-2 / WEIGHT: 200 POUNDS

Legendary University of Alabama coach Paul "Bear" Bryant called Joe Namath "the greatest athlete I've ever coached," and later Jets owner Woody Johnson called him "the most important player in the history of this franchise." Namath was not only a football star, he was also a league maker. Namath's decision to sign with the Jets instead of the NFL's St. Louis (now Arizona) Cardinals in 1965 brought the AFL credibility it had not previously achieved with sportswriters or fans. Soon, New York fans packed Shea Stadium for Jets games, the local press expanded its coverage of the AFL, and television ratings for AFL contests soared. When Namath upheld his guarantee of victory in Super Bowl III, NFL owners began to see the economic value of merging the two leagues. On the field, Namath had a lightning-quick delivery and a cannon arm. "He could throw a ball through a wall," said Jets center John Schmitt. Off the field, he was treated as a celebrity of the highest order and was once paid $10,000 to shave off his mustache for a shaving cream commercial.

The Heidi Game

The Jets' 1968 season featured not only an unexpected Super Bowl victory but also two remarkable games against the Oakland Raiders. The Jets won the more important contest—a come-from-behind victory in the AFL Championship Game. However, an earlier game that they lost became even more famous. The game took place in Oakland but drew a large television audience in New York. The lead seesawed back and forth until, with 65 seconds to go (and at nearly 7:00 P.M. in the East), New York's Jim Turner kicked what seemed to be the winning field goal. At least that's what Jets fans thought; they never got to see the game's final minute. Because the television network broadcasting the game had previously committed to show the family film *Heidi* at 7:00 P.M., it cut away from the game on the East Coast. New Yorkers never saw Oakland stun the Jets with two lightning-quick touchdowns to win 43–32. Outraged fans bombarded their local stations with calls. In a nationwide poll taken years later, football fans voted "The Heidi Game" as one of the all-time most memorable games.

FULLBACK MATT SNELL CARRIED THE BALL IN THE INFAMOUS "HEIDI GAME"

Joe's Promise

Jets fans had high expectations in 1968. The club had the league's top quarterback directing one of the AFL's best offenses, as well as a great defense led by end Gerry Philbin, linebacker Al Atkinson, and cornerback Johnny Sample. The Jets finished with an 11–3 record to top the Eastern Division of the AFL and advanced to the AFL Championship Game against the Oakland Raiders.

In a tight battle at Shea Stadium, New York edged Oakland 27–23, thanks to three Namath touchdown passes and two field goals by kicker Jim Turner. Namath didn't remember much of that game after suffering a concussion in the second quarter. Still, he led a late fourth-quarter drive for the winning touchdown.

The next stop on the "Jets Express" was Miami, where New York faced the NFL champion Baltimore Colts in Super Bowl III. Only die-hard New York or AFL

EMERSON BOOZER GAVE FUEL TO THE JETS EXPRESS'S SUPER BOWL RUN

Joe Klecko

DEFENSIVE TACKLE/END / JETS SEASONS: 1977–87 / HEIGHT: 6-FOOT-3 / WEIGHT: 263 POUNDS

Joe Klecko developed a special bond with Jets fans because, like many of them, he came from a working-class background. Klecko had worked as a truck driver and a boxer before attending Philadelphia's Temple University and starring on its football team. Because NFL scouts didn't regard Temple as a football powerhouse, Klecko was only a sixth-round pick in the 1977 NFL Draft. But he showed Jets coaches his talent as a pass rusher right away and was a starter at defensive end by the ninth game of his rookie season. Opposing blockers quickly grew to respect Klecko's strength and skills. Seattle Seahawks center Blair Bush said, "When Joe slams into you, we call it 'The Klecko Skate' because when he hits you, it looks like you're rolling backwards on skates." One of the most versatile defensive stars of all time, Klecko was the first player ever voted to the Pro Bowl at three different positions—defensive tackle, defensive end, and nose tackle. In 2004, Klecko joined Don Maynard and Joe Namath as the only Jets stars to have their numbers retired.

"In fact, I guarantee it."

fans believed the Jets had any chance. The Colts featured such future Hall-of-Famers as quarterback Johnny Unitas and tight end John Mackey. Some writers predicted the Colts would win by as much as 30 points. Namath had other ideas. "We're going to win Sunday," he boldly announced. "In fact, I guarantee it."

Coach Ewbank was furious after learning of the guarantee. "You can't go talking like this and giving the Colts fuel," he said. But Namath's words charged up his own teammates more than the Colts. Millions of fans watched in disbelief as the Jets scored first on a Snell touchdown, and their defense refused to budge throughout the game. The 16–7 Jets win was one of the most shocking upsets in sports history. It was also a turning point in professional football, proving that AFL teams were competitive and helping to pave the way for a merger of the two leagues before the 1970 season.

Jets fans were confident that Namath's arm could carry them to more titles. Unfortunately, his battered knees and injuries to other team leaders grounded the Jets. After joining the NFL in 1970, the Jets settled near the middle of the American Football Conference (AFC) standings. Namath remained a fine passer, and receiver Jerome Barkum and flamboyant running back John Riggins added power to the offense. But the club's record continued to slide.

When the Jets won a total of only six games in 1975 and 1976, the team's owners started making changes. First, a new coach—former Cleveland Browns linebacker Walt Michaels—was brought in.

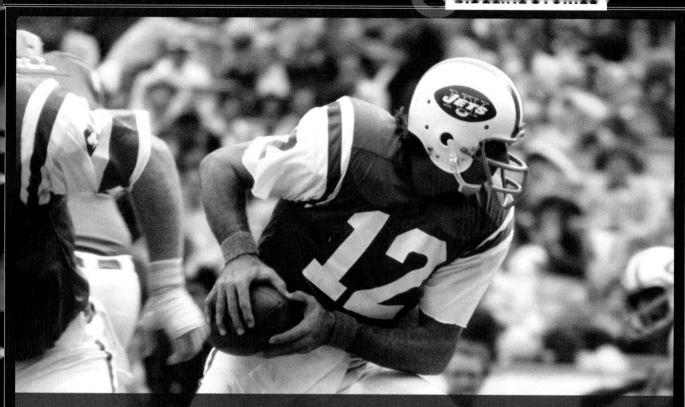

Namath's Bootleg

Joe Namath's guarantee before Super Bowl III was not his only daring prediction during his Jets career. He made another bold one midway through the 1974 season. The Jets were 1–7, and Namath's ailing knees were causing him to have a miserable year. Still, "Broadway Joe" predicted that the team would win its final six games and finish with a .500 record. Amazingly, that is just what the Jets did, beginning with an overtime victory against the New York Giants. That game featured one of the most unforgettable plays in team history. Trailing 20–13 late in the fourth quarter, the Jets had the ball on the Giants' three-yard line. Namath called a running play for halfback Emerson Boozer, but at the last second he surprised everyone by faking to Boozer and taking the ball himself in a stiff-legged bootleg to the left. Just as he limped across the goal line, two Giants players closed in, but Namath raised his arm as if to say, "Don't touch me," and the defenders held back. A few minutes later, the Jets won the game in overtime to start their six-game winning streak.

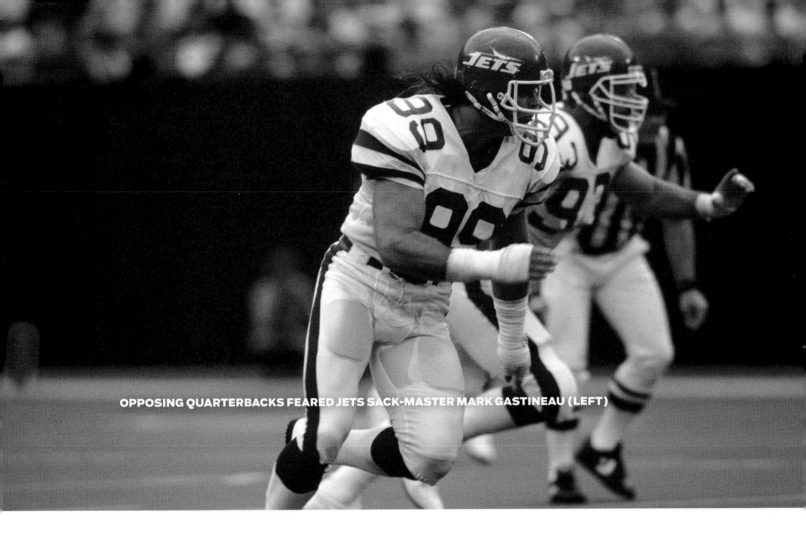

OPPOSING QUARTERBACKS FEARED JETS SACK-MASTER MARK GASTINEAU (LEFT)

Michaels turned the offense over to young quarterback Richard Todd and released Namath. Broadway Joe ended his New York career with more than 27,000 passing yards and 170 touchdowns—club records that still stand today.

ichaels's Jets, featuring Todd and defensive ends Joe Klecko and Mark Gastineau, began revving up Shea Stadium crowds in the late 1970s. Klecko and Gastineau joined with defensive tackles Marty Lyons and Abdul Salaam to form a hard-rushing defensive line nicknamed "The New York Sack Exchange." Gastineau earned both cheers and jeers when he celebrated his sacks by dancing over the fallen quarterback. Outraged owners of other NFL teams soon passed the "Gastineau Rule" to outlaw such showy celebrations.

In 1981, the Jets reached the NFL playoffs for the first time. In the opening round, the Jets fell behind the Buffalo Bills 24–0, made a remarkable comeback, but finally lost 31–27. Coach Michaels wasn't discouraged. "If all of New York hasn't fallen in love with this team yet," he said, "then they will in 1982."

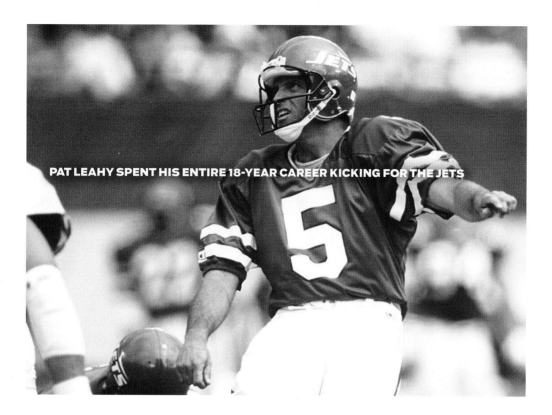

PAT LEAHY SPENT HIS ENTIRE 18-YEAR CAREER KICKING FOR THE JETS

The 1982 Jets advanced all the way to the AFC Championship Game before losing 14–0 to the Dolphins on a muddy field in Miami's Orange Bowl. Michaels retired after the loss and was replaced by Joe Walton. Before the 1984 season, the club moved its home base across the Hudson River to Giants Stadium (which Jets players and fans preferred to call "the Meadowlands"). Fans filled the larger stadium with even louder shouts of "J–E–T–S! Jets! Jets! Jets!"

The loudest cheers were reserved for quarterback Ken O'Brien, halfback Freeman McNeil, and wide receiver Al Toon, who led the club back to the playoffs in 1985. Fans became even more excited in 1986, when the Jets got off to a 10–1 start. Then O'Brien, Klecko, and several other key players went down with injuries, and the Jets lost their final five games, limping into the playoffs. They made a great showing in the postseason, however, first defeating the Kansas City Chiefs and then taking the Cleveland Browns into double-overtime before losing 23–20.

The Jets then seemed to lose their winning altitude and slipped down the AFC standings for the rest of the decade. Even the outstanding efforts of Pro-Bowlers such as safety Erik McMillan and tight end Mickey Shuler couldn't halt the slide. After a miserable 4–12 season in 1989, Walton was fired.

Learning to Walk Again

At 6-foot-5 and 275 pounds, defensive end Dennis Byrd (pictured) was big and powerful. He seemed destined for NFL stardom until November 29, 1992, when his career came to a crashing halt. Playing against the Kansas City Chiefs at the Meadowlands, Byrd and fellow defensive end Scott Mersereau rushed Chiefs quarterback Dave Krieg from opposite sides. When Krieg slid forward, the two defenders collided, and Byrd slammed his helmet into Mersereau's chest. While fans stood stunned, Jets trainers stabilized Byrd's broken neck before putting him on a stretcher, probably saving his life. For the next week, Byrd lay in a hospital, totally paralyzed. Then doctors noticed a slight movement in his big toe. The good news was relayed to Jets players before the start of their next game against the Buffalo Bills. They responded with a 24–17 upset win and later delivered the game ball to Byrd's hospital room. Through months of hard work, Byrd learned to walk again. Following his recovery, Byrd established a camp near his home in Oklahoma to help improve the lives of physically challenged children.

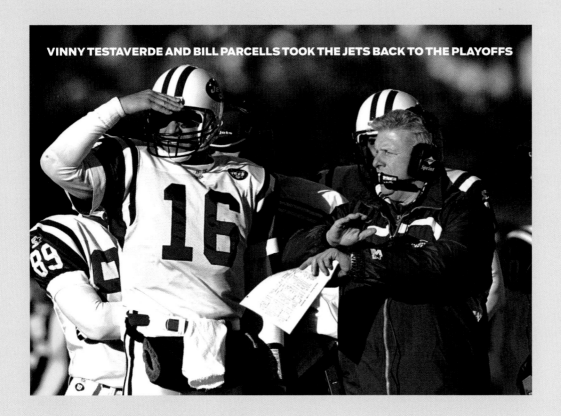

A Big Apple Rebuild

The Jets made it back to the playoffs in 1991 but took another nosedive in the two seasons that followed. After yet another losing campaign in 1994, team owner Leon Hess announced, "I'm 80 years old, and I want results now. I'm entitled to some enjoyment from this team, and that means winning."

Hess then made a disastrous decision, turning the club over to former NFL tight end Rich Kotite, who had recently been fired as coach of the Philadelphia Eagles. The easygoing Kotite had trouble enforcing his rules on players, and the Jets plummeted to a 3–13 record in 1995. "This is about as bad as you're ever going to see," Kotite remarked at the end of the season, but he was wrong. The next year, the club managed to win only one game. Kotite was then replaced by a man who knew a lot about winning in Giants Stadium, former New York Giants coach Bill Parcells.

Parcells was a legendary football figure in New York, having coached the Giants from 1983 to 1990 and led them to Super Bowl victories in 1986 and 1990. After a

OUTSPOKEN RECEIVER KEYSHAWN JOHNSON BEGAN HIS CAREER WITH NEW YORK

Wayne Chrebet

WIDE RECEIVER / JETS SEASONS: 1995–2005 / HEIGHT: 5-FOOT-10 / WEIGHT: 188 POUNDS

Wayne Chrebet had everything going against him when he asked the Jets for a tryout during the summer of 1995. He was smaller than most professional wide receivers, had played at tiny Hofstra University on New York's Long Island, and had not been drafted by any pro team. In fact, when Chrebet showed up for his first Jets workout, the team's security guard didn't want to let him in. But what Chrebet had going for him was his incredible courage: he was not afraid to run pass routes across the middle of the field, where huge linebackers and safeties might crush him to try to dislodge the ball from his hands. Amazingly, Chrebet not only made the team in 1995 but became one of its offensive stars for 11 seasons. By the time he was forced to retire after suffering a series of concussions, Chrebet ranked second in the Jets' record book in receptions, third in receiving yards, and third in touchdown passes caught. A favorite in New York, scores of fans showed up to games wearing his number 80 jersey.

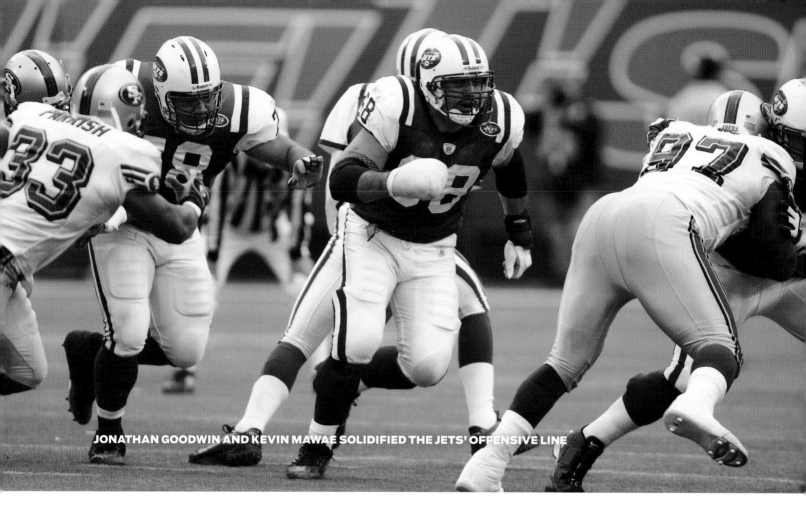

JONATHAN GOODWIN AND KEVIN MAWAE SOLIDIFIED THE JETS' OFFENSIVE LINE

three-year attempt at retirement, he had then returned to the game and transformed a broken-down New England Patriots team into a Super Bowl contender. Hess now offered Parcells a new challenge back in New York.

Parcells's lineup featured two key offensive weapons: receivers Wayne Chrebet and Keyshawn Johnson. The two were as different as night and day. The 5-foot-10 Chrebet was quiet, steady, and tough—more of a hard worker than a natural athlete. At 6-foot-4, Johnson was tall and smooth. He was also talkative and flashy.

Under Parcells's magic touch, the Jets jumped to a 9–7 record in 1997. The coach promised his players that even better times lay ahead. "I told them that nobody could stand still," he recalled. "You either get better, or you get worse. It's that simple."

To improve the team's chances, Parcells signed three free agents—running back Curtis Martin, center Kevin Mawae, and quarterback Vinny Testaverde. The new arrivals helped turn the Jets into an offensive powerhouse in 1998 and led the club to its first division title since its AFL days.

In the playoffs, the Jets defeated the Jacksonville Jaguars 34–24 to reach the AFC Championship Game opposite the Denver Broncos, the defending Super Bowl champions. In the title contest, Denver capitalized on six New York turnovers to crush the Jets' Super Bowl dreams 23–10.

Parcells stepped down after the 1999 season and handed the coaching reins to former assistant Al Groh. Groh led the Jets for only one year before resigning to become a college coach, but he made a key move that would brighten the club's future—selecting quarterback Chad Pennington in the first round of the 2000 NFL Draft.

The Jets were impressed with Pennington's accurate throwing arm, his commanding size (6-foot-3 and 225 pounds), and his intelligence. Pennington sat on the Jets' bench for two years until new coach Herm Edwards put him in the lineup midway through the 2002 season. Under Pennington, the Jets rebounded from a 2–5 start to finish the year as AFC East Division champs with a 9–7 record, putting them in the postseason again. Pennington's poise

CHAD PENNINGTON PASSED THE JETS INTO THE PLAYOFFS IN 2004 AND 2006

"Ha-ha-ha!" howled the crowd.
The pig tumbled down and trotted away.

The suddenly bald assistant turned to Aziz.
She stared. She **g**lared. Her nose **f**lared.

"Do you even know my name?" she snorted.
"My name is Zaza, and I can spell too."

Presto! Zaza snatched the wand.

Shazam! She turned Aziz's **h**at into a **b**at.

The bat flew around in z**i**gs and z**a**gs.
"Eeek!" cried the crowd.

Aziz grabbed the wand.

Presto!

He turned the ba**t** into a ba**g**.

Zaza seized the wand.

Shazam!

She turned the b**a**g
into a b**u**g.

Splat! went the bug beneath Zaza's foot.

Aziz twirled toward the t**i**p of Zaza's toe. *Tap!*
He turned the **b**ug to a **r**ug, to a r**a**g, to a ra**t**, to a **c**at.

"**M**eow!" sang the cat.
"**Y**eow!" howled Zaza.

With quick flicks Zaza turned
his **c**oat to a **g**oat, to a **b**oat, to
a bo**o**t, to a boo**k**, to a **r**ook.

"Caw!" called the rook.
"Raaaah!" roared the crowd.
"More!"

Presto!

He turned her bea**d**s into bea**n**s.

Shazam!

She turned the beans into . . .

The bears began to walk toward Aziz and Zaza.

Grrrrr!

The crowd gasped.

The bears were so close that Aziz and Zaza
could feel their hot breath.

They both held tightly to the wand.
"I was a **c**ad," he whispered.
"I was just **m**ad," she sighed.

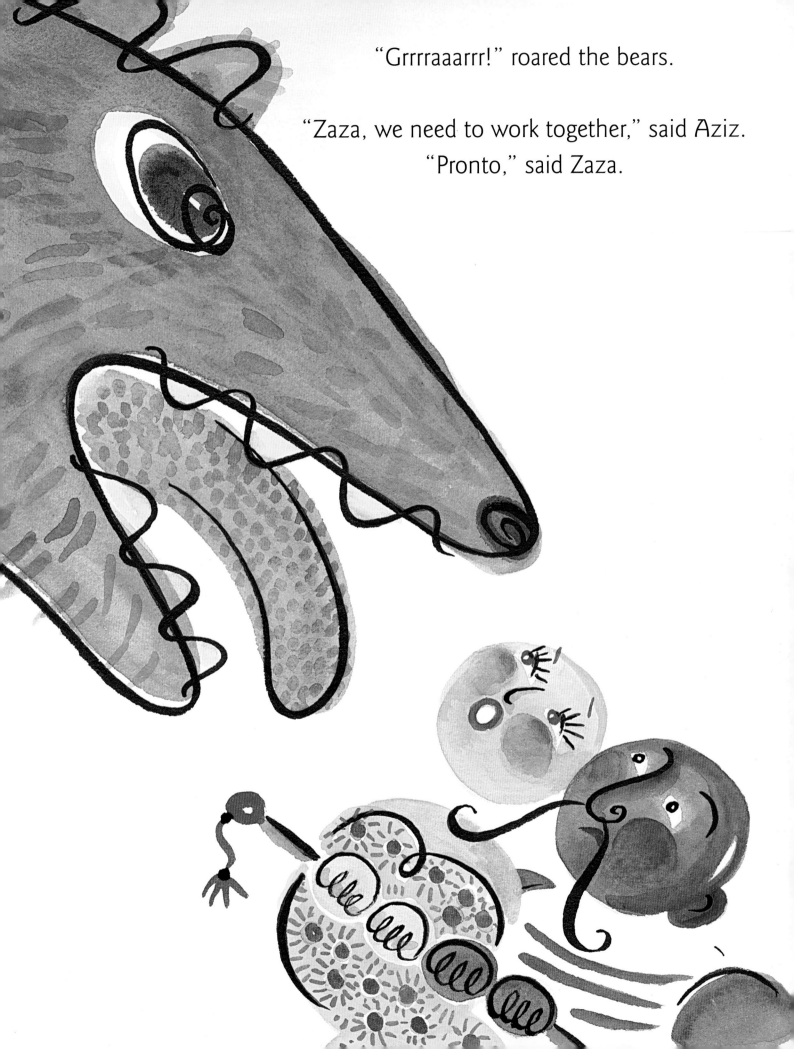

"Grrrraaarrr!" roared the bears.

"Zaza, we need to work together," said Aziz.
"Pronto," said Zaza.

Presto!

Aziz pulled out a card.

Shazam!

Zaza turned the c**a**rd to a c**o**rd.

Together they tied up the bears.

Ta-da!

Then, together, they took a big bow.
"Hoora**y**! Hoora**h**!" cheered the crowd.

From then on Zaza and Aziz shared the **l**ight each **n**ight.
Everything turned out just **r**ight.